BE TRUE
TO YOUR HORSE

BE TRUE
TO YOUR HORSE

"Deepening the Human-Horse Relationship"

DAVID LEE ARCHER

Edited by
Nicki Branch

To order additional copies of this book, contact:
Xlibris Corporation
1-888-795-4274
www.Xlibris.com
Orders@Xlibris.com
26225

CONTENTS

For all the people who believed in me,
For Ray and Rosalee,
For my best friend and companion
Smokey Joe.
For Buddy Hollo,
And mostly,
my Noello

♦ ♦ ♦

PREFACE

Some people were put on this earth with an inherent ability to communicate intuitively with horses. These individuals have a magical and almost mystical presence about them. To watch them walk across a dirt arena they walk with flowing grace. These rare gifted horse trainers are the best friend a horse can come across, for they understand them like few humans ever will. I met David Lee Archer at a clinic he was giving in California. He turned unwilling, wild, and behavior problem horses into mounts that were relaxed and listening to his every wish. I had never witnessed such a transformation in horses all within hours or even minutes. His communication was so subtle it was hard to perceive, but the horses listened to him and gave him their trust. David trains with natural leadership, asking the horses to move wherever he asks and to watch him work one is like watching a dance.

For several years now people all across the country have asked David to write a training book. A true cowboy who would rather be in the saddle day after day, writing a book was not on the top of his list of daily activities. The demands from people came more frequent though so he wrote down as best he could his methods for training horses. I worked with David for a year and finally got most of his techniques down in print. Enjoy his methods, for they work easily with horses. There is no better horseman that walks the face of this earth in my opinion, nor a kinder or gentler man. He is as genuine as the day is long and would give anyone the shirt off his back or his last nickel.

Bless you David, for sharing your incredible horse understanding gift with the world. Thank you for all you have given to the horses throughout your life, and all you have sacrificed so that you may be with your best friends in the world, horses. You have helped people understand horses better, improving their lives. I am genuinely grateful for helping with this training book which will allow others to utilize your methods so that they may make the incredible journey with their horse an easier path to follow on the road to oneness.

Nicki Branch, Editor

TRUE BEGINNINGS—DUSTY

As I sit here with my cowboy hat tipped back and glasses on, I think about how my cowboy days started so many years ago. It was with a little sorrel pony named Dusty. If someone were to ask what the biggest influence in my life was, I would have to say it was him.

It was through Dusty I learned many things, from what not to do, to the correct way to handle a horse. To me Dusty was as pretty as any horse out there, even thou he was blind in one eye.

We did all the adventures a boy could imagine with his trusty steed. When I was eight years old I had little Dusty doing the prettiest slides you could see. I would wet the grass and after doing a slide, would measure how long the slides were. Once I saw grand-prix jumping event on TV. Right after that I went outside, set up jumps, got on Dusty and tried to jump him three foot high. Poor little Dusty was only just over three foot tall himself. Nevertheless, he would give me his all trying to jump what I asked him. A couple of times he made it over and I can still remember that feeling I got as we cleared.

One time I found an old baby carriage, one of the ones that were large. I got some clothesline and made a harness for Dusty and hooked him up to it. I climbed into the carriage and off we went. The little guy never spooked, even as the carriage hit the backs of his legs. Years later our neighbor at the time told me she was watching me and Dusty going down the road in the carriage. She was amazed that Dusty didn't bolt or spook at the thing.

All the time I was riding Dusty he was a stallion. We didn't end up gelding him until years later. In time, I out-grew Dusty and starting riding normal sized horses. But every once in awhile I would go out in the meadow, jump on Dusty and ride around the pasture. I rode him the same as I had in the past, bareback with no bridle and no saddle, just my legs to guide him. Dusty taught many children how to ride through the years.

Sadly, I lost Dusty too soon. He escaped one night during a rain storm, got caught in a neighbors' electric fence and died. I buried Dusty the next day by hand, crying with each shovel of dirt. I was a young man of sixteen at the time. Dustys spirit is still deep within me. I have to say with all of the horses that I have ridden thru the years, none of them compare to that little pony except one, my appaloosa Smokey Joe ranks right up there with him.

My love for horses actually began years earlier before Dusty came into my life. The very first remembrance I have about horses is my dad taking me to pony rides. They weren't like the pony rides of today. It was a roped off area and you rode around on the pony between the ropes so you got the real feel of riding a pony. If you didn't make the pony move, it would stop. I do have to say I have my Dad to thank for where I am at today. He truly encouraged me with the horses and my family did go without so I could have horses.

I remember one time we were visiting some family friends and I was about five. I was riding a little black and white pony and he bucked, most likely not hard because I didn't get thrown. But from that day forward I was truly hooked on horses. Not long after that Dusty did come into the picture. That is where the foundation came in for me. Dad taught me to ride by putting me on Dusty bareback and without a bridle. We would go around in circles and got in all three gaits. This taught me balance and gave me confidence.

As the years went by we got the next horse who named was Trixie. She was an unbroken pony cross at the time and from an old horse trader we went and picked her up. He told my Dad that the horse was going to hurt me. A month later the horse trader saw me riding her. He pulled up and told me he couldn't believe it. That is when I found out what he told Dad.

Later on we bred Trixie to an Appaloosa stud and she had a little colt who I named Scout. By this time I was riding some horses for the horse trader. What was funny was the horse trader called me Robert for years. It wasn't until I was in my twenties that I told him my named was David. He looked at me and said "you mean you have been letting me call you Robert for all these years?" My response was "yes, you are my elder so it wasn't my place to correct you". He thought that was the greatest thing he ever heard.

Through the years I taught Scout a number of tricks, everything from bowing to falling down at a run. You have to remember I was a young kid who enjoyed watching westerns.

David and Scout in classic form.

At the age of fourteen or so I worked with a man by the name of Mr. Smithpot. I learned alot from him. Of course back then I didn't realize it. I learned little things from his daughter also like leg cues. We were working a horse named Jodie. She was a bad bucker but she wouldn't do it all the time. Looking back at what I know now, I would say she was in pain somewhere. To ride her you had to know a few things like ways how to keep a horse from bucking. What I am fixing to say might sound little strange, but you have to remember I was only fourteen at the time and very impressionable. Jodie and I were at a show and for the first couple of events she did well. Then she did her bucking thing. Mr. Smithpot walked to his truck and got his spurs, handed them to me and told me to put them on. He said, "Next time she bucks, just hook her and ride it out." At that moment I was one proud little boy. Proud of the fact he trusted me to ride a horse with spurs, and that he knew I could ride out the buck.

Today of course I wouldn't do it that way. But Mr. Smithpot at the time was seventy five years old and he had a lot of good ways, but you have to remember that was the way it was done back then. As the years went by I got the reputation of being able to ride any thing with four legs. I would ride any horse if asked to, and also I was known for having horse sense.

I went into the Air Force and that is when I got a chance to ride in the rodeos. My event was bareback riding, which I did just for the fun of it. Through the years I have been around and everywhere I have been horses were there. I never stuck to doing just one thing with them. I am just as happy on a jumper or working cows.

I don't even know how many horses I have ridden, I'm sure in the multitudes of thousands. Many times I have gone without material needs just so horses could be in my life. But the horses have given so much back to me also. I have been on several TV shows and have written for a few horse magazines. But the main thing I have found is that if you handle a lot of horses and a variety of breeds they will keep you honest with yourself. They will show you your shortcomings and also your strengths.

Also there is the spiritual side of horses that I keep to myself. I have met a lot of good people thru horses. I will say this. If some of you want to become a trainer, you have to be willing to give your all and remember you won't have a life any longer as you know it. Sometimes it is really hard, but then that one horse comes to you and you get to see that horse change. Then you know it is all worth it.

To me working with horse is like working with people. Just be honest with them and know their shortcomings and yours. In turn it will make them a better horse and you a better person.

Looking back at my life at fifty years old, I have seen many changes in the horse business, some good and some not so good. I have seen the so-called "new" training methods which if the truth were known, these methods aren't really new, they just have a fancy name put to them.

My key thing is to just be honest with the horse and treat it as a horse. Horses can't love us like humans do, and they also are not a dog, as some folks think. They are a horse, nothing more and nothing less.

I hear so many times how a horse is reacting because they are scared of being eaten as prey. Well the truth is, at one time humans also were nothing but prey animals. So think about it. When we get scared we aren't scared because we think we are going to be eaten, we just react with good old human instinct. We are not thinking "something is going to eat us."

A domesticated horse has not had to worry about something eating them for a long time. So when horses react, it is just that—a reaction. It is called equine instinct. To me, believing that a horse thinks that way is not being honest with the horse. Some people like using that term though because it is more dramatic to hear.

Training a horse is something that is a seven day a week job. You must learn to read the horse and also to recognize when you are in over your head with a horse. Training horses takes patience, persistence and purpose. People also should realize that each and every time they put a halter on a horse it is a training experience for that horse. No matter how well the horse is trained, a person can undo a good horse by making training mistakes faster than it took to train it the first time.

Due to the abundance of horse training programs in the market now, people unrealistically think all they have to do is take a course and they can become a trainer. Realistically, it takes years and a variety of horses to really become a good horse trainer and even with time, some people just don't have what it takes to become an effective trainer.

As you read this book ask yourself if you really have what it takes to work with a horse. As long as you are honest with the horse, they will be honest with you. Like I said before, remember that a horse is and always will be a horse. They also have a heart, a soul and a brain. This is not just a how-to book on horse training. I have put a lot of myself in this book, my personal feelings about horses, and life in general. To me, it all ties together as one. We exist in this world together, all creatures both large and small.

THE UNSPOKEN LANGUAGE

Since a horse is a non-verbal animal, you have to first realize they communicate through body language, smell and hearing. In this chapter we are doing to be going thru the different aspects of each one.

The main type of language a horse uses is body language. Have you ever noticed that when a person walks up to a horse and the person is timid, the horse gets nervous? The horse is sensing and absorbing the humans' emotions and body language. If the human is tentative, the horse will start to look around and wonder why this other animal near them is nervous, and in turn they will become that way. If a person walks up to the same horse and is calm and confident in themself, the horse will stand there calmly.

For example, a woman unloaded a horse from a trailer and the horse was nervously moving back and forth while being led. She was leading the horse by walking with timid steps and her arm stretched out. I went over and took the horse from her, made it back up, and walked lazily off with it. The horse then led nice and relaxed and wasn't any trouble for me. The woman had been nervous, which in turn made the horse nervous.

There are six parts of the horse's body I work off of. Number one is the flank area. If I walk towards the flank area I want the horse to move. I use a plastic bag on a stick to ask the horse to move off. I will walk towards their flank area and if they don't respond I bring up the plastic bag (will be referring to it as a flag). At first, the horse might move quickly away from the flag. Keep doing this until the horse moves away relaxed.

Next I move to the shoulder area. I position myself between the horses' shoulder and their jaw line and walk towards that area. If the horse doesn't move, I will put my hand on the neck and push. But I try to do this with as little pressure as possible. Each time you do this, use less and less pressure until the horse will move with out you touching them at all.

Also I will work the front part of the shoulder. I want the horse to back if I walk towards the shoulder. Here you will be using the flag again. I will take a step towards them and if the horse doesn't move I will wave my flag as hard as it takes for them to respond. At first, they will move to the side as they take a step back. That is fine if they do, as long as the feet are moving at first. In time, the horse will start moving straight back. Once you get where the horse is moving nice and relaxed on one side then move to the other and do the same thing.

Always start at the flank area first. That helps them get the idea of what you are asking. Asking the horse to move off your body helps build the leadership you need to have with your horse. It also helps the horse learn they can relax around you because you are in charge. All of this moving off the body work is done "in hand", and what I call working a horse "in hand". In other words you will only have a rope halter and lead on them.

At this point you might be wondering, "What if I don't want my horse to move?" When we are asking something of our horse, our body posture is different. We will stand more erect than if we were just going up to the horse to pet on them. Our body language changes when asking different things of a horse and we don't even realize we are doing it.

This is where we start putting the foundation on the horse. Many times you can fix some bad behavior problems in horses by doing just these simple in hand exercises, as long as the behavior problem did not come from the horse being in pain. Always investigate the pain issue first with a behavior problem horse.

I once got a call from a woman who could not get a bridle on her horse. I drove to her place and noticed right off the bat that the horse was spoiled. First, I checked the mare's teeth to make sure there were no sharp points on them. Many times bridling problems stem from teeth which need floating so I had to rule that out. Then I felt the mares' poll area, between her ears, to make sure she wasn't sore in that area. Her poll was fine, so I went in with my flag and the owner asked "How come you aren't taking the bridle with you?" I just smiled at her and said, "Watch." By using the flag, I got the horse working off my body easily and in a relaxed state.

Then I asked the owner to hand me the bridle. At this point she was really looking at me strangely. I put my hand on the horses' head and she lowered it easily. I then slipped the bit in the mares' mouth, pulled the headstall right over her ears and there was no resistance at all from her. This episode took only a few minutes and showed the owner what you can accomplish, in this case fixing a bridling issue, by working your horse in hand and having it move off your body. By working the horse from the six points of its body, I am establishing myself as the leader in the horses mind. It all goes back to treating a horse as what it is, simply a horse, who only speaks horse language and nothing else.

One thing that really bothers me which I see happen over and over again in this business, is certain personality types of horse owners who are in fact detrimental to the long term well-being of horses. There are some individuals who are always going to be nervous around horses. This is the owner that seems to find the perfect horse, then soon afterwards the horse does something wrong and the owner sells it. They then find the next perfect horse, usually an impulse buy, and same thing happens again. Too much horse they say, or they didn't like this or that about it and sell it, and the search goes on. If you find yourself going to through several horses, you need to honestly ask yourself if it's a horse you really want. Maybe it would be better to get dog instead. They are smaller and less intimidating. I have seen too many times where a person decides to by a horse because of the wrong reasons. The poor horse at the end pays for it by being shuffled from owner to owner through no fault of its own.

The second way a horse has to communicate is thru smell. Have you ever wondered why your horse acts as if they don't like certain people who they have never been around before? I feel like it has to do with the horses' sense of smell. It has been proven that when a human gets upset or nervous, their body chemistry changes, produces pheromones, and a horse can actually smell the difference. That is one of the ways a horse can tell if a person is nervous or fearful around them.

Hearing is not as important as the first two equine senses, body language and smell. Tone is more important than anything to a horse though. When working with horses if you find yourself talking to them, keep your tone nice and even.

I was once doing a clinic and one of the riders was always yelling at her horse. The more she yelled, the more the horse got nervous. I watched her when she was around her husband and she did the same to him. I worked her horse and the horse did well. I brought the owner into the round pen with her horse and showed her how to work with it. I ended up telling her she needed to stop yelling all the time, that her horse doesn't appreciate it and she is not accomplishing anything except making the horse nervous. She denied yelling at her horse. So I then looked over at her husband and told her "You need to stop yelling at him too. There are other ways of getting your point across to communicate". Hopefully she took my advice.

Just remember, when talking to your horse, to keep it nice and pleasing to the ear. It doesn't matter so much what you say, but more importantly how you say it.

HALTER TRAINING, STARTING YOUR FOUNDATION

I have found that putting a foundation on a horse starts at halter training. When halter training is done right, everything else falls into place. Taking these simple steps will help you to have a better relationship with your horse. You just have to remember the three P's as I call them. They are Patience, Persistence and Purpose. I will be going into more detail about the body work with the horse in this chapter.

Equipment you will need is a rope halter, a twenty-five foot lead or lunge line. I prefer a round cotton one. The reason being if something happens, it is less likely to get wrapped around a horses' leg. You will also need a lunge whip and a flag, or attach a piece of plastic on a stick or on a broken whip.

You don't necessarily need a round pen to get started with your horse. if you have a small area you can work them in, that should work. The area should be at least twenty four by twenty four feet.

When training a horse to halter, no matter if it is a weanling or a two year old, I always start them the same way. Before I put any forward pressure on the halter I start by driving them forward. I start close to the flank area. I am using the whip to move the horse forward while also using the flag to keep horse turning into me. The main thing is to watch your body position and stay at the flank area of the horse. The horse at first might react to the flag and move off quickly. Don't worry, they will start to relax after a short time.

When the horse starts to move forward, let more line out. At the beginning I said you need a twenty five foot line. A good rule of thumb is to use one longer than the radius you are working in. That way, if the horse gets away from you, you still have plenty of lunge line. I use forty five foot cotton lines since I work in a sixty foot round pen.

Here I am flexing his neck towards me.
I also step in front of his shoulder to encourage him to turn.

Here he is bending real well and I am asking to move his front end towards me.

In this photo I am starting to teach the horse to disengage his hind end.

The next step I work on is getting the horse lighter on the halter and I will teach the horse how to cross over on the front end. If you notice everything I am doing is going to come to play later down in the training.

I will take my lead behind the hind quarters as shown above. The horse might move off quickly when he feels the lead on his hind quarters. Just make sure you keep the line right above the hocks.

I am draping my line on one side to the back of his hocks.

I will keep doing this until the horse starts to relax and starts to give to the halter. It doesn't take long until the horse gets real light as shown in the below picture. Notice the slack in the line. At this point all I have to do is just too lightly bring the lead into play and the horse will turn towards me.

If you notice I haven't put any forward pressure on the horse yet. That is the next step; also remember to work both sides of the horse. I work one side just as much the other. I don't work on the stiff side of a horse longer. If you do that you will have to go back and work on the horse good side because it will end up getting stiff. So work both sides the same, the horse will get light on the stiff side in time.

Here as you see just like on the right side, he is soft on the left side also. The most important thing is that I put more pressure on him he will turn towards me and not move away from me. He is telling me he is learning what the pressure from the halter means.

Since now the horse has an idea what the halter is, I don't have to worry to much about him rearing or going up in the air when he feels the halter on his poll when I ask him to walk towards me. The next shot you see me pulling on the horses lead. Now as soon as he gives to the pressure I will let him have some slack. I don't care if I get one foot at a time.

Even though I am facing the horse, I will not look into the horse's eyes. If I do that, the horse will freeze on me. I will keep this up until I can ask the horse to move forward with a light touch.

In this picture I am asking him to move forward. Here again, look how much slack I have in my line.

When the horse starts to give to the halter and come forward real well, I will refine it to the point that I can ask the horse to move just one foot at a time. When the horse is leading good, I will try to get the horse to the point where each foot step of theirs will match with my footsteps. I want them to be so tuned in to me that if I stop in mid-stride, they in turn will stop in mid-stride.

The next step will be to ask the horse to move backwards. At first I will take his halter and push him backwards and with my flag I will move it down low at his legs as shown below.

I want to get the horse to the point if I just walk towards the front part of their shoulder the horse will back up.

After a time, I shouldn't have to really put any pressure on the halter when working the horse in hand. To me the halter is just there if I need it. The key thing is to keep working on each step until the horse does it willingly and relaxed. Also, don't over-school on the horse on the in-hand work. If you do too much, the horse will sour and not want to work for you. I don't work a horse in liberty until the horse works well in hand. I want to control his movement. I don't want the horse to learn when I first start working him he gets to run around. I don't really do much lunging. I know a lot of people lunge just for the sake of getting the horse tired, but I want to train a fresh horse. I want them to learn that I can just crawl in the saddle and get to work.

If you do all these steps properly, when it comes to teach the horse to tie, you will be surprised. Most horses will end up just standing there tied as soon as they feel the halter because they know what pressure from the halter is.

What the horse learns at this point is going to come together in the end. The horse is going to learn how to move from pressure, how to cross over on the front and how to disengage his hind quarters. Also he will learn how to flex at the poll laterally and vertically.

The foundation is very important. If you get lazy and miss a step, somewhere it will come back to bite you in the behind. It all falls back to leadership, which if you don't have, you will not have the horses respect. Without respect, when you try to teach the horse to do everything from working off its hind quarters to loading in the trailer, there will be a fight. That is not being fair to the horse or true to it. Like I said, be true to your horse. They need Leadership. With Leadership, you will find you have a much more relaxed as well as happy horse.

I have found people in horse training circles are always looking for a easy quick way and try to take a short cut. Just as in life, working with horses there are no short cuts.

I don't do much liberty work with my horses and that is a personal thing. For one thing, I have had horses in for training and the owners brag about how the horse will work in the round pen. Yes, the horse does work well in the round pen, that is until you put a lead on it and they don't have a clue what to do.

After I do the first few steps I will start working the horse back and forth. I ask them to move forward then at first I will step towards the shoulder with the flag in hand and encourage them to turn. I will try to use as little pressure as needed. But if I have to get there and really wave the flag hard at first I will do so. When they start responding to the flag well, I go to my lunge whip. Here I want the horse to get to the point where if I lay the end of the whip in front of them they will easily change directions. I will do this until I can get the same result just with my arms. This will fine tune the in hand work. Get them to a point that if you just put a little pressure on the lead they will turn and go the other way.

You can do this with horses that are already started under saddle. It will help them be more responsive.

I will be repeating myself a lot in this book. I want to really drive home to be true to the horse and let it be a horse. You have realize ever time you put a halter on the horse you are training it.

I try to approach a horse as I do life. Realize there will be some bad days and also that there will be some good ones. With every bad day, at the end you will have many good ones. Just as with raising kids, I like to try to let the horse think for themselves. Just give them the direction that they need. If we get out of the horse's way most of the time they will make the right choice.

This type of ground work is very important because it is putting a good foundation on the horse. You are teaching the horse how to move away from pressure, and it is learning to give at the poll. Plus, you are building the working relationship you need.

All of my horses can sit for a long time without being ridden, and when I go and get one to ride I don't have to lunge it first prior to climbing in the saddle. I might work the horse a little back and forth with the reins after its tacked up, but then I just climb on and ride. I am able to do that because they have the right foundation on them. Here is a good example. Some one wanted to go trail riding one day. I went and got my old mare Lady who really hadn't been ridden in three years. She had been busy with having babies when I used to breed. I was asked if I was going to lunge her prior to riding. I said "No, I am not." They then asked "Aren't you worried about her bucking?" I said "No, I am not." So I got on her and off we went for a nice trail ride. This is because Lady was given the proper foundation at the beginning of her training, a lasting impression on the horse.

PERSONAL THOUGHTS

                I have been around horses in some shape or form all of my life. They are a very important part of it. I have worked so many, several thousands, that I have forgotten many of them. As always, the super good horses and the real rank ones always stand out in my mind though.

Horses are just like people in the way that if they have a problem, all they need is to be given a chance. Many times someone has called and said "Everyone is telling me to put my horse down." Then I go work with the horse, find out how it ticks and go from there. I will end up having the owner working the horse plus having fun with the horse instead of putting it down.

When I look into horses' eyes I see their spirit. There is nothing like the feeling you get when you are working a problem horse and all of a sudden you see their eye soften up and they are stuck to your side. They are matching every move you make, and it is like dancing with them. You can lead a horse and every footfall of theirs is matching yours. If you stop in mid stride they will also. That will give me goose bumps, as much as putting a good spin on a horse.

One of the problems I am seeing in this industry is some trainers are doing things just so they can give the people what they want to hear or see and help them to sell tapes. Don't get me wrong. I think it is great that someone is making money doing what they like to do. But the problem I am seeing is that no one is honestly being true to the horse. You have to remember a horse is never going to love you as a person will. If we were to die tonight and not be there for the horse in the morning, the main thing they would miss is the food we throw to them.

That is not saying you can't build a special bond between you and your horse. When working the horse properly the horse will call to you even if you aren't the one feeding it. They like the companionship, but once again it isn't love as we know it.

I have heard it all in the years past. I even heard someone say to me "My horse wont let me saddle him because I didn't tell give him a hug and a kiss and tell him I love him." I was thinking at the time well that is why he won't let you saddle him. I have notice this happens mostly with women owners. I am sorry, but that is the truth. Some women treat their horse as a boyfriend or something. But a horse is no less or no more than a horse, something special in their own right, so we need to treat them as such.

Instead of trying to get the horse to love you like a human, try letting yourself be true to the nature of the horse. In that way, and only that way, you and the horse will become one. When you finally get that done and can jump over a fence with out a saddle or bridle, just you and the horse, then you will know what I am talking about. To me that is a most special place. The freedom you feel when doing something like that is really something. Yes, it takes commitment and time to work with your horse the right way, but it doesn't take as long as you might think. But if you are giving your horse treats and letting it walk all over you and then thinking how you can get that horse to love you, you will never be one with the horse. All you will be is the two legged creature that he gets to push around and have no respect for.

If you aren't willing to put in the time . . . you will never have a true relationship with your horse. If you send your horse to a trainer, you still have to put your time in working with your horse. It doesn't do any good to send one to a trainer if you don't know how to follow up with what they did. I will tell a future customer if they aren't willing to work with me don't bring the horse to me. I don't want them to waste my time or their money. I have done it in the past but it doesn't work very often. So now I won't even consider taking a horse the owner won't work with me with. Even if they say they are good horsemen, I still say no.

I have found that people will not always be truthful when it comes to how much they know about horses. I received a call one time about a horse years ago. The owner said that she use to train and rode a lot, but hadn't ridden in a long time and wanted me to start her horse, so I did. I took the horse back and she wanted me to ride it before I left. I asked for a saddle blanket and a saddle and she looked at me and said "What is a saddle blanket?" I looked at her in disbelief, and so I rode the horse. Later I put her on top of the horse. In just a very short time I knew all of this was a mistake. I asked her to get off of her horse looked her straight in the eye and told her how I felt.

Sometimes folks are so busy trying to be something they aren't that they loose out in life and love. They have the mindset of "what about me?" and their life is spent searching for ways they can get more for themselves at all costs. The thing with that kind of thinking is they lose out on so much. Those types of people will go thru life thinking about what they can get out of life, instead of what they can give, and they end up loosing. They will never find true happiness.

I think we should all try to look at people and life as if every day were our last. Even working with our horses, do it as if it is the last time we ever get to work and enjoy them. At times, yes, it is hard to have that mind set. But funny thing is if you find yourself drifting from that frame of mind and go back to it, everything always seems better and goes smoother.

Someone said something to me about how long ago they remember when horse people would help other horse people freely, without bringing money into it. I also remember those days with fondness. Personally, I think we were better off then. I remember riding tons of horses and never getting paid, never even thinking to ask for money. I thought I was lucky to be just doing what I loved.

I personally wish I were able to just go around the country helping horses and their owners and not even have to worry about getting paid. I feel like it isn't about us or the money, it's about helping the horses and their owners have a happier life.

People in the horse industry seem to be getting the mind set that if you don't believe and train as they do, then you are wrong. In life, sometimes there is no exact right or wrong. We need to start excepting things as they are, not as we want them. If we can do that, the world would be a better place.

BUILDING CONFIDENCE IN YOU AND YOUR HORSE

"There is always light at the end of the tunnel"

Now we are going to be working on you and the horse's confidence. These are simple things to help build the trust and leadership you need with your horse. Also this helps with building that foundation you want in your horse. These are just few exercises to do, the key thing is to be inventive. Come up with as many things to work with your horse on the ground and it will pay off on the trail. I go through all these steps, even with my problem horses. Many times I will fix a certain problem by doing these steps.

Take the case of a rearing horse. Now I am not talking about the one who will flip themselves but the mild cases. By doing these steps that I had in the previous chapter and this one, it will help relax your horse in the neck and poll area. I have found that many horses that rear have never been taught to relax. I am working a mustang right now who I call "the boxer." He liked to strike with his front feet if you tried to put a halter on him. Just by doing these steps I was able to stop him from striking. Because by doing these steps I taught him that I was his leader, and I was in charge. It is simpler than you think, but you still have to put the time with the horse.

I will work the horse back and forth until they get light in the halter and I just have to gently touch my line and they will turn. Also, this helps them to learn to cross over on their hindquarters or the correct term is to disengage the hind end. Some horses I will use a broken lunge whip, which I am using here, or I will use my flag.

It all depends on the horse. The rail helps me to turn the horse. When the horse gets light then I will move in the middle of the round pen. If you don't have one you can do this out in a big area also. Now when working the horse back and forth, make sure you put them on the circle some so they don't get soured.

When the horse starts to give nicely to the halter and working back and forth on a loose line, then I teach them how to give to pressure with my lunge whip. Here I have Patience side passing and learning how to cross over.

I start out gently tapping. If I don't get a response I tap a little harder. But make sure you reward the horse if they try. Some people put the horse facing the rail. I personally teach them out in the open. If the horse is light on the halter as they should be I can control the forward movement with out any trouble just by putting a little pressure on my line. Now notice my body position. I am not standing in front of the horse but to one side.

From there I will start adding things into the picture. Here I am using a mounting block. I consistently get asked how to get a horse to stand still next to a mounting block. Here's a perfect way.

All I do is the same as I did on the ground but I just stand on a mounting block. I work the horse back and forth and bring it in a little closer each time. I make sure and pet on them to reward them and let them rest a minute. Also, if a horse has never been ridden before, this helps to get them use to something being above them. I am going to say again make sure you put them back on the circle a little, and not just keep on going back and forth all the time.

In this picture I am working Patience a little closer to me.

When the horse is getting relaxed and is trying, always make sure you reward them. In the next picture below you will see how teaching a horse to give to pressure comes in handy.

I am using my lunge whip to move Patience's hind end over to the block.

When she gets close I will make sure I rub her neck and withers and tell her
what a good job she has done.

From there, we go to the bridge and do the same thing. I position the
bridge about a foot away from the rail at first. As the horse gets used to the
bridge I will move it closer to the rail. In the next picture Patience is
jumping the bridge. I just keep working the horse back and forth until
they will step on it nice and relaxed. Here is a good tip, as soon as your
horses' hind end passes the bridge, turn them back towards the bridge.

On the top picture Patience is standing nice and relaxed on the bridge, so I make sure she stands there and I pet her. I will let her stand there so she learns that is her resting spot. I did the same with the mounting block. Whatever a horse spooks at, I try to work them and then let the rest next to whatever the object was that spooked them.

Now I do the same thing in the middle of the round pen as I did with the mounting block. From there, what I will do is have the horses' front feet on the bridge and get them to move their hind quarters over, so then they will be pivoting on the front end and I can get them to go all the way around the bridge without ever stepping off with their front feet. In the next picture I am asking Patience to move her hindquarters.

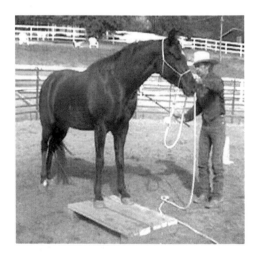

You can use different things with your horse and approach the objects the same way. If you have barrels lying around, teach your horse how to walk over them and not jump them. Also, you can use tarps. Make it fun for you and the horse. Challenge their mind and yours, and remember, the more you do at the start, the better foundation you will put on your horse.

A COWBOYS JOURNEY

It all started many years ago now. A cowboy was at his wits end. Nothing seemed to be going right in his life. He felt like his world was coming to an end. On a whim, he called a visionary to find out where his life was heading. The visionary told him he would move south and encounter a woman who wasn't what she seemed to be. The visionary also told him you must make the move because it will eventually lead to better things, even though at the time it won't seem like it.

Then the visionary told the cowboy he would be moving to California. She said when he first goes there, it will be to teach something. The visionary had no idea the cowboy did clinics and knew he worked with animals, but not necessarily horses.

The cowboy told her "There is no way I am moving to California, I have heard about those people out there". The visionary insisted and said "Yes, you will be living in California. On your journey, you will be meeting a Shaman and he is going to play a major part in your life. Since the cowboy had some Navajo and Cherokee blood in him he liked that idea.

Years went by. Yes, the cowboy did end up moving south to work horses. In time, he started to do more clinics and everything started to fall into place. Even the woman who wasn't what she seemed to be was the reason he got to go to California because she booked a clinic for him.

The cowboy had a yearning for something more in his life, but he never could put a finger on it.

As soon as he stepped off the plane the first time he landed in California, he had a feeling come across him like he never felt before. He looked around and thought to himself "this is where I belong." In time he moved to California and his life turned with major changes for the good. He met a wonderful lady and lots of nice people.

The cowboy forgot about how he was supposed to meet a Shaman. He and his lady bought a ranch in a pretty little valley in southern California.

Together, they rescued horses from across the country and trained them. When they started to buy their hay by the truckload and stacked it near the barn, the cowboy noticed funny things started to happen at the ranch. He was seeing things that weren't really there, ghostlike images. Hay would fall off the truck mysteriously, and his dog would bark as if barking at a person while there was nobody there.

The cowboy has raised all kinds of animals throughout his life. He never had a problem saving all kinds baby animals. Strangely, nothing that was just real young at the ranch would live. He lost a few young animals all under the age of one. First a two month old miniature colt coliced, then died after the surgery. Then a premature calf was born on the property which died later while being bottle fed. Three peacock babies had also died when brought home to the ranch. They were distraught with grief over the losses and couldn't help but think that babies were not allowed to live there.

The cowboy and his lady had adopted a crippled wild burro from the BLM several months prior. They found out she had been bred in the wild, and was expecting. Fearful they would lose another baby and since ghostlike presences were being felt on the property, they researched the Native American Indian heritage in the area of the ranch. Three reservations were nearby, so the cowboy called one and asked for a Shaman to come out to the ranch and told him what he was experiencing.

A few days later the Shaman showed up with two other Indians. They brought sage and an eagle wing fan. Well the story starts to unfold at this time. The Shaman told the cowboy that a baby had died long ago in a certain spot on the property, and the haystack was placed on top where he was buried, also near where the family's dwelling had been. The Shaman also said that the ranch was sitting on what used to be an Indian village. He then prayed with the other two Indians in their native tongue, lit the sage, fanning the smoke, and did a cleansing ceremony to bless the ranch. During the ceremony, the horses ran around in their stalls, bucked and jumped, and one of the ranch dogs was barking wildly in the doorway of the barn as if something were there. The Shaman told the cowboy things he couldn't have known, such as where the ghostly images were sited and which direction they moved.

After the Indian blessing was over, the cowboy was told by the Shaman to move the haystack, and also a pen where the ponies were housed, as they were on sacred spots that were bothering the spirits. Crazy as it sounded, the cowboy knew it had to be done and moved the haystack then the building with a truck and tractor. He did everything exactly as the Shaman told him to.

During this time, the cowboy got very sick with the flu, but he still worked hard for three days and did what needed to be done. The day he finally finished moving everything, he all of a sudden felt better. In the process of cleaning some things up on the ground, he found proof, Indian grinding tools and rocks, artifacts that there was a village there which backed up Shamans' story.

Since then, the cowboy found out through historians that there was much bloodshed around the area because the white men wanted the Indians' land, and whole tribes were slaughtered. The cowboy learned more about the local Indian culture, the Luiseno and Pala, and made several more friends who return to the ranch. He has been adopted by some of the local Native Americans as a brother. The wild burro delivered a healthy baby jack who was christened, Jiminy Wakan Tengalkat, an American-Sioux-Luiseno name.

If you think about it, it's a shame what has happened to the Native American Indians in the past. We took their culture away from them and their language, all for the sole reason to make them more like the white man, instead of respecting them for what they were and learning from them. The white man had to conquer instead.

So now the cowboys' vision told many years ago to him came true. But the journey still goes on, because the circle never ends and the real journey is just beginning. No matter what our race, we need to learn we are all brothers and sisters. Also all creatures are special, no matter how small or how big. If we practice that, then the world would be a better place. We should show respect to all living animals. Of course we first we have to respect ourselves.

I have seen to many times how we blame other people for our actions. After a time, it is up to the individual to change their life and stop putting the blame on someone else. People sometimes turn to drugs and alcohol to hide from themselves and their problems, but in reality, it just makes things worse. I hope when it is time for me to meet the great spirit in the sky, I will leave this world a better place. That is all we can do. Worry not so much about the time we have left on this earth, but how we can use that time.

THE FIRST SADDLING

The first saddling is where you really have to be careful with your horse. For one thing, this is where the most accidents happen to the horse and person. Remember to take things one step at a time.

Equipment needed:

1. Half inch cotton rope 30 feet long with a o-ring on one end.

2. Saddle pad

3. Saddle lightweight

4. Halter and lead thirty feet long

5. Coat hanger

Before you get started, take the coat hanger apart and straighten it out. But leave a hook on one end.

I do all this with the horse in hand. Start with the cotton rope. Take it around the barrel of the horse and run the other end thru the o-ring. Using the cotton rope can get the horse used to pressure around the barrel without using a saddle. Pull the rope so you have pressure on it, which is around their girth area.

Make sure you are standing away from the horse in case they react. Each time you pull try to put more pressure on the rope. Do this standing, then at a walk, trot and a canter with the horse, holding the leadrope in your left hand and girth rope in your right. Keep working on this until the horse is relaxed with the pressure.

I have seen all too often where someone will saddle up a horse and just let the horse buck it out. Then an accident happens and the saddle is hung up on the horse. Instead, by doing this in hand with a lead rope and halter on the horses head, we can control the horse better. NEVER saddle a horse for the first time and just let it run around with out being able to control it.

For example, I had a horse in for training that was deathly afraid of saddles. His ingrained fear came from a bad saddle experience the very first time he was saddled many years ago. He got into trouble because he was allowed to just buck it out free. He got tangled in the saddle and was traumatized. Now he trembles at just the sight of a saddle. This poor boys' post-traumatic shock could have been prevented just by having a safety line on him properly.

When the horse is relaxed with the pressure of the rope around the barrel we can now introduce the blanket to it. Never just walk up to the horse with the blanket held high. Keep the blanket low and just slowly touch the horse in shoulder area and work your way to their back. When they let you set the blanket on their back, start to rub the horse with the blanket. Get to the point where you can even bring the blanket over the horses' head and they just stand there. I like to do this until I can stand about three feet from them and throw the blanket on their backs. While doing this step I usually have the saddle in close by so the horse has a chance to see it and smell it.

When the horse is relaxed with the saddle pad it is time to introduce the saddle. If the horse is nervous when you first pick up the saddle give the horse a chance to smell it. Once in awhile the horse will back up from it. If the horse is backing slowly away from the saddle just continue to slowly walk towards the horse. When the horse stops, rub the horse on the neck. If the horse is relaxed, attempt to put the saddle on. Make sure everything is up and on top of the saddle. Put your stirrups on the saddle horn so they won't fall and hit the horse.

Set the saddle on the horse easily, don't just throw it up there. Try to bring it up high and gently lower the saddle and when it is on the horse's back go back to rubbing the horse. Walk to the other side and bring down your girth and stirrup. Always keep one hand on the lead line so you can control the horse.

Take your coat hanger and grasp the girth and bring it to you. After you have the girth, rub the girth area with your hand. When you tighten the girth make sure it isn't too loose or too tight. You don't want it so loose the saddle will move and get under the horse accidentally. And having the girth too tight all at once is going to make the horse really react and want to buck, so just make it snug.

Now step away and ask the horse to move, if the horse bucks try to keep the horse from getting into trouble by controlling its head. At this point you might want to have a flag or something in hand so if the horse comes towards you, you can keep the horse off of you. When the horse is moving relaxed, stop it and tighten up the saddle a little more.

Ask the horse to move off again. Stay at this until the horse is going easily in both directions at all gaits without reacting to the saddle. Also I will at this point make the horse move back and forth, changing directions quickly.

From this point on, every time you work the horse go ahead and saddle them up, even if you are only doing ground work.

BITTING UP YOUR HORSE

This is an important part of how your horse is going to handle you being in the saddle. I have seen many problems caused by not starting the horse right on the bit, everything from rearing to bucking.

The key thing is like everything else, don't get into a hurry. Start off with just rubbing the bars of the mouth where the bit sits with your finger. That helps the horse to get used to something going into his mouth, plus it is a pleasurable experience to them.

Either start out with a full-cheek or a O-ring snaffle bit for your horse. I use both, and to be honest it is just what kind of mood I am in. I go back and forth but I lean more towards the O-ring. When using a O-ring make sure you have a chin strap on the bit. The chin strap is just to help keep the bit from sliding into the horse's mouth.

When I put the bit into the horse's mouth the first time I make sure my bridle is over sized. That way I can slide it over the ears more easily. Even on my finished horses I always have my headstall a little bigger and then when I get the bit in the mouth I adjust it. I adjust the bit so it is just touching I don't want any wrinkles. I try to look at it as if someone is putting something in my mouth how I would want it.

Back to the bit I know a lot of people will go with a rubber covered bit. Here is a personal experience I had many years ago. I decided to go with the rubber snaffle bit. I had about four training horses I was working all at the same place in training while I was training part time back then. Well they all had head problems. I wondered what I was doing wrong. I couldn't come up with anything, whenever I have a problem I am the first place I look. Many times people create their own problems without even realizing it.

I figured out that I wasn't doing anything wrong. All the horses' teeth were fine with no sharp edges. I called an old timer and told him what was going on with all my horses having head problems and I told him what kind of bit I was using. He told me to put the bit in my mouth and see how is tasted, so I did. It was nasty tasting. So I went back to my old sweet iron snaffle that I am still using today. All of the horses' head problems went away as soon as I changed bits.

Before we put the bit into the horses mouth, have the teeth checked by your vet, dentist, or you can do it yourself. Take your finger and put it into the horses' mouth and take your finger towards the meat part of cheek. Now pull your finger out of the mouth and run it down the upper teeth. If you feel any sharp points, have your horses teeth floated before you bit them up. If you don't get the horses teeth floated and they have points on the teeth you are going to create problems.

I have seen horses even buck because of sharp teeth. I was doing a clinic and there was a horse there that was a bucker and was throwing her head. The people just bought the horse a few weeks before. The tip off to me on the problem with the horse was the throwing of her head. They brought the horse into the pen for me to work and I did a little flag work with the horse at a walk and got the horse moving off my body in a nice relaxed mood. I then jumped on the horse with nothing on her, no bridle or saddle, just had my flag in hand. That mare worked like a champ. We cantered and did figure eights and all I was using was my body and flag to control the horse.

I climbed off the horse and put a halter on her and had the owner to come in. I showed the owner how to check the teeth. Come to find out this mares teeth were really sharp. I later heard from the owners after the horses teeth were floated, everything was fine and they didn't have any problems with her anymore. I can give you tons of examples of things like this where many horses' problems were caused by sharp teeth.

Now we are ready to put the bit into the mouth. Take your right hand and told the top of the headstall and take your left hand and hold the bit. Put your right hand over the poll the area between the ears and gently pull the headstall towards the horses' ears. When the bit gets close to the horses' mouth, take your index finger and rub the bar of the mouth before you slip the bit in. That will encourage the horse to open its mouth. Now if the horse backs up just back up with them. Do not make a big deal out of it if they back and don't stop, just keep walking with them.

When you get the bit in the horses' mouth, let them wear it for awhile before you go pulling on it. What I do is some groundwork and let them carry the bit and get used to it in their mouth. When they stop chewing on the bit then I will start adding pressure to it. Start on one side stand at the horses shoulder and take your rein and pull their head towards you. At first as soon as they move their head a little let your rein go slack. Each time try to hold their head a little longer. We don't want to try to flex them all at one time.

Do this until you can flex the horses' head towards you with little pressure. Also they should hold their head there until you pick up the other rein. Now here is the key idea to this exercise. If you feel like you are holding the horses head with the rein and feel the weight of it, you are not ready to go to the next step yet, so you have to keep working at it. Too many times I have seen where a person might thinks they have the horse light on the bit when in fact they aren't.

Now we are ready to ground drive the horse. If you did everything and didn't miss a step this is going to just fall into place. This where the horse will tell you if you missed something along the way or not. Remember from the start we began right off with teaching the horse to bend laterally. We also got the horse use to something on their legs and behind their hocks.

I use round cotton ropes to ground drive. Do not use flat lunge lines. Flat lines can wrap around the horses legs, tighten up, and injure them if something happens. Use anywhere from twenty-five to forty foot lines. I use a western saddle all the time even to line drive. After I get a horse used to being saddled no matter what I am going to be doing with the horse I saddle them up.

When using a western saddle take a short rope and tie it to one stirrup and take the rope under the belly and tie it to the other stirrup. Run your driving lines thru the stirrups and up to the bit. When I start off line driving, I do it at a walk. Now when you first ask the horse to move off, if they get into a hurry don't do any thing bu let them come down to a walk on their own. But if you didn't miss any previous steps they should pretty much just walk off easily.

I start them on the rail and like I said at a walk. I will turn them into the rail a few times until I feel them getting light on the bit, then I will start turning them into the center. I would start this in a small area, and it doesn't have to be a round pen.

When the horse is responding at a walk, I will put them into a trot and just like at the beginning at the walk I will turn them into the rail few times then I will start and try to do figure eights with them. At this point I might even have some ground poles on the ground. At the trot is when I start working on my stop also. At first I will put them into a trot on the rail and ask for a stop verbally and at the same time I will turn them into the rail. I will use just one line when doing this at first and slowly bring in the inside rein when I see the horse start to respond.

The horse now is driving well at a walk, trot and stopping well. Now we go to a canter or a lope. We ask for a lope and as the horse is loping along the rail, try to bring them off the rail a little towards you and then gently turn them back into the rail. When line driving the horse at a lope, I don't do figure eights. I use the lope more for teaching a fast stop.

Remember we already taught the horse to stop at a trot. So right here is when we really start putting a good stop on a horse. Now we have already taught the horse to give to the bit at a lope no now we will basically do the same thing to teach the horse to stop quickly at a lope. Put the horse a little closer to the rail and verbally ask for a stop and turn them into the rail but not all the way to make a turn just enough to get them to stop. When you see the horse responding, bring in the other line. We keep doing this until if we just increase the pressure a little the horse will stop.

If you get the horse real light on the ground it will help to make that first ride go well.

THE FIRST RIDE

By this time the horse should be used to the bit and saddle and know how to give to the bit vertically as well as laterally. Before I get into what to do next I will say this. If you are not a good rider DO NOT try to ride the horse for the first time. With some horses, no matter how much preparation work you do, they still might buck on that first ride. Therefore, I recommend two people for when you first climb into the saddle.

Some people when they put the saddle on pick up a stirrup and drop it so the horse gets us to it. I do it differently because a horse will react different to it when moving. I will ask the horse to move forward from the ground. I take one stirrup in my hand and start tapping them in the side with the stirrup so they get the feel of the pressure there while they are moving. Do this on both sides and keep at it until the horse will move faster if tapped. In other words I will ask the horse to walk forward. Then I tap to ask for a trot. If they don't trot I will tap again but this time a little harder. I want to get the horse where if you just tap them once in the side with the stirrup, they will move forward.

Now, I usually will bring in another horse that I will ride and pony the horse with so the horse gets used to someone being above them. This is where some of the foundation you worked on earlier will come in. If you did some of the groundwork from mounting block they are already used to something above them a little. Now if you don't have another horse to do this with, you can sit on the rail and just work the horse back and forth from the rail. Get the horse up close to you and when it is close, rub on the horse to get it relaxed with you being above it.

You can take as long as you like doing this. If you want to really get the horse used to you being above it, go ahead and take a few days doing this. Now that the horse is relaxed with you being above them, it is time to get them used to some weight.

From here you can step up in the stirrup from the ground or use a mounting block. I do both it mostly depends on the horse. If I have a real tall horse I don't want to be pulling on the horses back or tapping them with my toe when putting my foot into the stirrup. I just step up and then down again. I keep doing this until the horse is fine with it, nice and relaxed.

With the weight part I will just lay across the saddle with the horses' head pulled towards me. If the horse tries to move off and I know it is just a little side movement that is not going to be a fast move, I will keep laying across them until they stop moving and only then step down to get the weight off of them. At this point even when I am stepping up into the stirrup I will turn their head a little towards me. You always want to control their hind end so if something happens you can move their butt away from you. You must do both sides of the horse. I am of the habit I mount on the left but on my green horses I will dismount on the right. I want a horse that will let me get on any direction I wish. Now once again don't get into a hurry let the horse tell you when it is time to go to the next step.

When the horse is relaxed with all of this and is consistent, it is time to bring the other person in.

Now is it important the other person knows when to back off of the horse and read its body language well. Let the other person work the horse from the ground a little so the horse gets used to them.

The rider mounts and the person on the ground slowly asks the horse to move forward. Start out by doing small circles both ways. Remember when you turn the horse in the other direction they will react as if they don't know what you are asking.

When the horse is moving relaxed at a walk, then have the ground person ask for a trot. But once again do not push the horse too hard or too fast. Just trot off a few steps at a time, and each time try to trot a little farther. Most horses I will just ask for a walk and a trot the first ride. Now slowly the rider takes over and starts asking for the walk and trot. If the horse is little fussy about going into the gait have the ground person step in and ask for it. Do this until the rider can take over completely.

About when to ask your horse for a canter, I wouldn't ask for a canter until the horse is used to the rider real well. They must be able to walk, trot and stop well. Also take some time to develop their mouth. When you ask for that first canter just try a few steps at a time. Put them into an extended trot, hold them into it and they usually will go into a canter. Remember, you get what you put into it. If you try to cut corners in training a horse it will show. Take your time and don't be in a hurry. The better foundation you put on your horse the better off and happier both of you will be.

REFLECTIONS

As sit here on this cold rainy day there are two pot bellied pigs at my feet. Yes, I said pot bellied pigs, but that is another story. Writing this book brings up alot of things in the horse world and in my life to mind. I have seen a lot of so-called changes in the horse training world as far as techniques. But in reality they aren't changes, just people being more educated and informed. Most of the training methods that are being taught nowadays have been around for a long time.

The round pen is a good example. I was reading a book that was published in the late eighteen hundreds. It said for a problem horse to put it in a corn crib and run it around until it starts to come to you. Now a corn crib is round for those who don't know. Instead of trainers keeping their secrets to themselves, they are now starting to share and show some of the training methods they use.

As you have noticed in the past pages I keep on saying about treating a horse like a horse and respect them for what they are and not for what they aren't. I have seen where people either try to treat a horse like a boyfriend or girlfriend or also like a dog. That is when people start getting into trouble. Those folks have good heart but just don't realize what they are doing. On the flip side of this industry you have the people who treat horses as if they are machines who don't really care about the horse being a living creature. Even some top trainers think that way. I overheard a conversation one day where a top trainer who trains cutting and reining horses and someone asked him about him starting eighteen month olds under saddle so they can be shown as a two year old in cutting and reining.

He was basically asked if he was worried about the horse not holding up. His response was the horse is either going to be at stud or having babies by the time it is three so it doesn't matter. That kind of mindset bothers me.

But if you think about it, we do it to our kids also. Let's say you have a boy who is a talented baseball pitcher. I have seen where they keep pushing the boy hard through high school. But by the time he is eighteen, the boys arm is already injured and he never makes it to the major leagues.

When training horses, I try to go at it as if I were a horse and how I would want to be treated. I let them make mistakes and try to let them think for themselves. I respect a horse for what it is. To me it is a very special animal. I have the personal privilege of it letting me ride it. Lets face it, if a horse really didn't want someone on their backs, they could easily get rid of them.

As I tell everyone, remember, a horse has a heart, a soul and a brain. Horse people are a different breed. Some people give up material things so they can just be around horses. That commitment is for the love of the horse. There is something about horses that stirs up deep emotions in people. That love is what brought me to horses my entire life. They are my existence, in my heart and my soul. They are my family.

We should try to work in unity with the horse at all times. When I do in-hand work with the horse sometimes I listen to music playing and it is as if the horse and I are performing a dance to the music. Their every move is matching my every move and we are in time with the music. I do the same when I am riding the horse.

You can have that special relationship with a horse just by treating a horse like a horse. You don't need any treats to bribe them and you don't have to beat them into submission. Just enjoy the horse for what it is, a horse, no more and no less.

DEVELOPING A SOFT MOUTH

Many times I see people and horse problems because nobody took the time to develop a horse's mouth the right way. Either they get a horse where they will have a hard mouth or they get a false give. What I mean about a false give is the horse doesn't truly know how to give to the bit. They will do it at a walk and maybe a trot but if you try to get them to give to the bit at a lope they will push out on the bit. It happens when someone works on the giving from side to side. But what they do is when the horse flexes, they let go of the rein. They don't wait until the horse will really soften and will hold their head in that spot. So many problems come from not teaching the horse to be soft on the bit.

Notice the hand position, pull towards your belly

It is a pretty simple process. I suggest using a o-ring snaffle bit for this. I use a three inch one that has sweet iron in the middle. I have tried all sorts of bits out and I keep going back to my o-ring bit.

I start at a stand still, pull their head to the side while my hand is pulling towards my belly button. The horse should turn its head towards you. When I feel that I am not holding the horses head up with my hands and I feel a little slack in my rein then I will let the rein go. I don't let the rein slide in my hand. I want to reward the horse completely by dropping the rein. Doing all this will help with the giving at the poll vertically also.

From there we start at a walk. Here we will be working not only on giving to the bit, but also disengaging the hind end or crossing over with the hind legs. We will be doing a one rein stop. At a walk gently pull one rein to your belly button. Hold your rein until the horse comes to a complete stop. This also will teach your horse to follow its shoulder. I see a lot where people who are direct reining and they pull to the side. A horse can still walk forward with their head pulled to the side. But by pulling towards the middle of your stomach it lefts up the shoulder and they have to follow the shoulder.

Each time when you are walking and doing the one rein stop just walk a few strides. I usually count to five then pull their heads to the side. Make sure you do both sides. Don't do one side more than the other. The horse will be stiffer on one side but don't worry about it they will get soft on that side. If you work more on their stiff side you end up getting the stiff side soft but the other side will end up becoming the stiff side.

When the horse starts to stop and is soft on the bit at a walk by doing the one rein stop you are ready for the next step. Now do this at a trot. If you are just about to ask for a trot and the horse trots sooner than you asked, make sure you get them down to a walk before you allow them to trot. You don't let the horse trot until you ask for it.

Doing this exercise will also help your balance and also with developing your hands. At a trot do the same as with a walk, just go a few strides at first. After you do this for some time, put the horse on the straight and at a trot just play with your one rein and you will find the horse will come down to a walk with very little pressure.

Now it is time to go a lope or canter. This is a good exercise for a horse that wants to get in a hurry at a canter. With doing the one rein stop on the count of five, the horse figures out there is no reason to get in a hurry because they are going to stop in just a few strides. You don't want to start this at a lope until the horse is doing well at a trot. If you do this too soon, the horse can loose their balance.

As always make sure you work the horse on both sides. Now after the horse is doing a nice one rein stop at a lope, go ahead and increase your count. But if the horse starts to get in a hurry, do a one rein stop right then. If you even feel like the horse is starting to get in a hurry make sure you stop them. A big mistake people make at a lope is that they do the one rein stop too late. They react to the horse instead of trying to feel the horse under them.

This is about the best training tool you can use. Don't get bored with it, keep working on the one rein stop. You can get the horse to the point that at canter you can just put a little pressure on one rein and you can do a sliding stop. Someone watching you won't even be able to tell you put pressure on the bit. I had a training horse and I could run full out and just by playing with one rein he would slide to a stop. Well the owner was riding him one day and he found out what I mean when I say sit deep. He ended up starting to use his hands for balance at a jog. Well the horse felt the pressure on one rein and came down to a slide. Needless to say since the fellows balance wasn't right he ended up on the horse's neck. The horse just did exactly what he was told.

Here the horse is trying to buck, but he is controlled easily by utilizing the one rein stop.

Every part in this book I talk about getting the horse so you can do things by using as little pressure as necessary. Of course first the horse has to learn what pressure means. But after they learn that, just play with it at all gaits. When doing in-hand work just try to use as little pressure as possible to get the job done. Same with giving to the bit. Keep playing with it until you can do everything with your pinky finger with the slightest touch. When you can get them that light then start using just your legs and body to cue them. You will be surprised what the average person can do if they just put the time and effort into it.

A MAN AND HIS HORSE

This chapter is about how my best friend and companion Smokey Joe and I came together. Smokey is a horse I will never replace.

One morning a man named Buddy Hollo went and checked on his mare since she was ready to foal any day. As he walked into the barn he saw something lying beside the mare and it was a grulla colt that he named Smokey Joe.

Smokey Joe as a baby.

As the years went by Smokey was used as a stallion to produce babies and he was just halter broke. The year Smokey was being born I was moving back to the Midwest. The years before Smokey and I came together I was showing horses, training, shoeing and had a full time job. At the time in my life when I first saw Smokey I was sort of in limbo. I really wanted to train full time, but in the Midwest that is hard to do and make ends meet.

When I first met Buddy we became good friends right off the bat. I found out my dad and his mom were real good friends in high school. We used to cook out at Buddy's alot on the weekends. I kept noticing the appaloosa stud in the pasture. I ended up breeding a mare to the stud who was Smokey Joe. One day at a cook out Buddy ask me if I wanted to climb on Smokey and I of course said yes. Well just as my leg was crossing his hind end, Buddy informed me that he only been on Smokey Joe for five minutes. Now knowing Buddy that meant he just put some weight in the stirrup. He was the type of person if you were riding next to him he would slip your headset off of the horse for kicks.

All went smoothly and after a short time I was working Smokey with just my legs. I told Buddy right then if Smokey ever came up for sale I wanted first bid.

As time went by every time I went over to Buddy's I would go see Smokey. One day I was over there shoeing some horses and Buddy was getting ready to feed. He started to tell me how when he would go in to feed Smokey he had to watch his back because Smokey would charge him with an open mouth. I didn't believe him because I never did see that in that Smokey. Buddy went to grain Smokey at this time and Smokey was right outside his stall so Buddy thought he was safe. Smokey came charging in the stall with teeth showing and Buddy had to jump over the stall door to get away from him. I must say it was funny to see.

One day the phone rang and it was Buddy asking me if I really wanted Smokey and I said sure. Buddy went into how it was shame his horse thought more of me that him. He told me how much he wanted for him I told him no, that I would give him more than that because Smokey was worth more. Buddy said no I just want you have him.

I went to pick him up and Smokey and I had a talk about how he can't charge me in the stall. You might be wondering how I did it. I simply poured some feed in the feeder and stood there with a flag in my hand and when Smokey came charging at me, I would scare him off with the flag and had him to stand next to the back wall. It didn't take long for him to realize who was in control. After that one time I could do whatever I wanted to him as he was eating and he didn't care.

The first few rides I had on Smokey had been all without a bridle. As a matter of fact for the next few months I would ride him more without one than with a bridle.

David riding Smokey bridleless on his fourth ride.

From that time forward Smokey set himself apart from other horses I had known in his training. His very first show he took a second in western pleasure and it was a big class. He was still a stud at this time but you would never have known it by his calm demeanor. One cold winter day someone went out to see Smokey and he was out in the pasture with some mares and a gelding. All the mares in the pasture were bred so Smokey didn't act studly to the geldings. I saw the people that night and they said they couldn't see Smokey. But they started talking about this appaloosa that followed them all over the place. I started laughing and told them that was Smokey. They couldn't believe it because he was so well natured.

Smokey and David doing a trick sidepass in 2003 at Day of the Horse Celebration, Valley Center, California.

Smokey turned out to be one of those rare and great horses you can do anything with. I have shown in him western pleasure, reining, team penning, cross country jumping and stadium jumping. He also can work a cow with the best of them.

While I was living in Tennessee, it got to the point at the Horse Fair everyone was expecting to see Smokey and I do our stuff. There is bond between him and I that can't be broken. One time I was getting my hair cut and the

lady cutting my hair who knew Smokey told me she had a buyer for
him who was willing to give me fifty thousand dollars for him. But
there was and is no amount of money that can buy him. He is my partner
in life.

Smokey I have to say is a ham. Once Buddy came and got him to breed
some mares. Well I have to say it didn't go well. Buddy and him never did
get along even after I bought him. I was helping a friend who was a disc
jockey for a country radio station who was doing a remote broadcast. Buddy
was taking Smokey back home and stopped by the station. So the disc
jockey asked the manager of the cowboy bar where we were at if we could
bring Smokey into the bar and the manager said sure. We brought Smokey
in and the disc jockey asked Smokey a question and Smokey whinnied out
loud as if on cue. So we ad-libbed it a little. Then the disc jockey asked
Smokey another question and sure enough Smokey whinnied again. I know
the people listening to the radio thought it was a set-up, but it wasn't.
Even when we do a free style when Smokey hears the music he is ready to
go to work.

*Smokey Joe and David on a cattle drive at Old Lilac Ranch, Valley
Center, California. 2003.*

It has been ten years now since Smokey and I came together and he has given me more than one heck of a good ride in life. He gave me the motivation to go forward when I needed it. I use him alot in my daily training of other horses, clinics, and for demonstrations. He is a gelding now, and great one at that.

So to Buddy Hollo my friend, I'd like to thank you up there wherever you are at for bringing Smokey and I together. I lost Buddy in 2003 at the age of fifty. I remember telling him once in our wild days that we have to grow up and he said he never would. This chapter is in his and Smokeys' honor. May we all have a horse and a friend as good as the two of them.

Smokey Joe as he is today, 2004.

CLOSING THOUGHTS

I have been into horses for over forty years. They have always been special to me and always will capture my heart. A horse is a very simple animal. They just want and need guidance. As horse owners we owe them that guidance and leadership. It isn't as hard as people believe. You just have to be true to the horse and to the way they think.

You give a horse what they need and they will follow you to the ends of the earth. We all can learn from the horse if we open our minds and hearts to them. As the Indians say, listen to the wind. Change the terms to listen to the horse and the horse will tell you when to go forward. You have to learn to look into their soul. If you aren't able to do that, then you will have trouble.

I am finding compassion is getting in short supply these days. Everyone wants to be an expert. But when dealing with horses there is only one expert and that is the horse. Does any human really know what a horse is thinking? No we don't, but we can read their bodies and get a good idea. If you open yourself up you will be able to tell the difference between a horses behavior problem versus a pain issue.

As I said in the book owning and riding a horse is a privilege and not a right as far as I am concerned. I have been with horses for a long time. You notice I said "with", I didn't say "own or train" them. When working a horse I feel like I should approach it like I am with the horse. In other words I want to become in the long run as if we are one.

I ride frequently without a bridle and just a line around the horses' neck. This isn't a big trick and isn't difficult to do. All you are doing is working off the horses' shoulders, just opening and shutting their shoulders. You still have to trust the horse. If you get a horse where you can just jump on their back and ride with nothing on them, it is just you and the horse, that is the best feeling you can get. The way I look at is the horse is allowing you to ride them without aides, just your body and mind.

As my Lakota Sioux brother says, the horse is a sacred animal. To me, all living things are sacred.

It has been many years since I climbed on my first pony named Dusty. I still can remember that feeling when we did our first slide and our first airs above ground. Yes I taught him how to at the age of nine. You can teach older horses anything as long as you know the mechanics of what you are teaching.

The problem is people for whatever reason feel like they have to control animals and people for that matter. It is hard for us to except things as they are for what they are. We do it with all animals and we also have done it to the Indians. For some odd reason we try to make people and animals into what we want them to be. The shame of it is we lose out so much by doing so. You are probably asking yourself what does this have to do with horses? Well it has everything do with horses. As I said before, accept a horse for what it is. Don't try to make it something it isn't. You will find the more you let a horse be a horse the more you will enjoy them.

For years many people have tried talk me into writing a how to book and I have put it off. The reason I did was that they were so many books already out there on training. But then I saw something was missing in all of them. It seems the public the last few years has been talking about natural horsemanship training. But what is natural? Having a rider on a horses' back isn't natural. Plus one interpretation of natural could be different than the next persons. All I mean by being to true to the horse is just being true to the horse's needs and each horse's personality and treating a horse like a horse.

I hope you have enjoyed this book and remember to be safe. A horse can be a dangerous if not handled properly. Always handle them with respect and dignity as the magnificent animal they are.

Enjoy your horse, learn from it while giving it leadership, and remember my motto, "Be True to Your Horse and They Will Be True to You."